That's What
FRIENDS are FOR

That's What FRIENDS are FOR

HALF THE SORROWS, DOUBLE THE JOY

BY BONNIE LOUISE GILLIS

Willow Creek Press®

Published by Willow Creek Press, Inc.
P.O. Box 147, Minocqua, Wisconsin 54548

Photo Credits:

p2 © Richard Du Toit/Minden Pictures; p5 © Glenn Bartley/Minden Pictures; p6 © Tui De Roy/Minden Pictures;
p8 © Masterfile Royalty-Free; p11 © Mitsuaki Iwago/Minden Pictures; p12 © H. Schmidbauer/Blickwinkel/age fotostock;
© Suzi Eszterhas/Minden Pictures; p16 Eastphoto/age fotostock; p19 © Patrick Keintz/Minden Pictures;
p20 © Shinya Sasaki/AFLO/age fotostock; p23 © Jan Vermeer/Minden Pictures; p24 © Mark Raycroft/Minden Pictures;
p26 © Raimund Linke/Masterfile; p29 © Doug Perrine/NPL/Minden Pictures; p30 © Rob Reijnen/NiS/age fotostock;
p33 © Ann and Steve Toon/ NPL/Minden Pictures; p34 © Tim Fitzharris/Minden Pictures; p37 © Theo Allofs/Minden Pictures;
p38 © Herbert Spichtinger/ImageSource/age fotostock; p41 © Sean Crane/Minden Pictures;
p42 © Sumio Harada/Minden Pictures; p44 © Jane Burton/NPL/Minden Pictures; p47 © Fotofeeling/age fotostock;
p48 © Benjamin Barthelemy/Minden Pictures; p51 © McPhoto/age fotostock; p52 © Tom & Pat Leeson/Leeson Photography;
p55 © Christina Krutz/Masterfile; p56 © Konrad Wothe/Minden Pictures; p59 © Gregsi/Masterfile;
p60 © Gerry Ellis/Minden Pictures; p62 © Mark Raycroft/Minden Pictures; p65 © Duncan Usher/Minden Pictures;
p66 © Jurgen and Christine Sohns/Minden Pictures; p69 © Gerard Lacz/age fotostock;
p70 © Donald M. Jones/Minden Pictures; p73 © Mark Taylor/Minden Pictures; p74 © Hiroya Minakuchi/Minden Pictures;
p77 © Tom & Pat Leeson/Leeson Photography; p78 © Nate Chappell/Minden Pictures;
p80 © Tom & Pat Leeson/Leeson Photography; p83 © Mark Raycroft/Minden Pictures; p84 © Xi Zhinong/Minden Pictures;
p87 © Jurgen and Christine Sohns/FLPA/Minden Pictures; p88 © Ingo Arndt/Minden Pictures;
p91 © Bill Gozansky/age fotostock; p92 © Willeecole Photography/Masterfile; p95 © Andy Rouse/Minden Pictures;
p96 © Yva Momatiuk and John Eastcott/Minden Pictures

Printed in China

COULD WE SURVIVE WITHOUT FRIENDS?
MAYBE IN THE SAME WAY WE COULD LIVE
WITHOUT LAUGHTER AND CHOCOLATE
AND CONVERSATION AND SMILES AND HUGS.
BUT TO KNOW THAT YOU'LL BE LOVED ON DAYS
WHEN YOU FEEL ENTIRELY UNLOVABLE,
THAT YOU CAN TRUST SOMEONE TO LOOK INSIDE
AND TO UNDERSTAND, OR FORGIVE,
THAT YOU'VE GOT SOMEONE TO
LAUGH WITH, TO CRY WITH,
TO DO THINGS WITH, AND DO NOTHING WITH,
THIS IS THE STUFF OF JOY—
AND THAT'S WHAT FRIENDS ARE FOR.

Friends ARE FOR COMFORT

FRIENDS HELP YOU TO FIND IMPORTANT
THINGS WHEN YOU HAVE LOST THEM...
YOUR SMILE, YOUR HOPE,
AND YOUR COURAGE.

—Doe Zantamata

FRIENDS ARE FOR
hugging
when it
HURTS

FOR
laughing
WHEN
nothing IS
FUNNY

for not
EATING out
ALONE

For NEVER
feeling
ALONE

FOR
cheering
UP A blue
DAY

FOR
wearing
A PINK
ribbon

for FINDING BRIGHT spots IN storms

FOR cleaning UP after STORMS

Friends ARE FOR COURAGE

IT IS NOT SO MUCH OUR FRIENDS' HELP THAT HELPS US
AS THE CONFIDENT KNOWLEDGE THAT
THEY WILL HELP US.

—Epicurus

Friends
ARE FOR
TRYING new
THINGS

For
LETTING
OLD things
GO

For FEELING
brave
IN
THE DARK

FOR
facing
FEAR IN THE
light

For
LEANING ON
each other's
STRENGTH

for STANDING
SIDE by SIDE

FOR
hearing
"YOU CAN
do it"

For not
HAVING
to DO IT
alone

Friends ARE FOR PERSPECTIVE

MY FRIEND, IF I COULD GIVE YOU ONE THING,

I WOULD WISH FOR YOU THE ABILITY TO SEE

YOURSELF AS OTHERS SEE YOU.

THEN YOU WOULD REALIZE WHAT A

TRULY SPECIAL PERSON YOU ARE.

—B. A. Billingsly

FRIENDS are for discovering A NEW point of VIEW

For
ENJOYING
THE *same*
view TOGETHER

FOR
connecting
WITH A kindred
SPIRIT

For SEEING
beauty IN
differences

FOR lifting EACH OTHER up

For KEEPING EACH other GROUNDED

For
CONSULTING
on FASHION

FOR
not GIVING
A DAMN about
fashion

Friends ARE FOR UNDERSTANDING

CHRISTOPHER ROBIN LOOKED LONG
AND HARD AT POOH'S FACE...
"ARE YOU LEARNING ME BY
HEART?" ASKED POOH.
"NO," HE ANSWERED, "I KNOW YOU BY HEART.
YOU ARE INSIDE MY HEART."

—A.A. Milne

FRIENDS are for DROPPING in without an INVITATION

For STICKING around when EVERYONE ELSE leaves

For KNOWING WHAT to say

FOR
knowing WHEN
WORDS will
do no GOOD

FOR
venting
UNTIL *the*
steam is
GONE

For CRYING UNTIL no tears ARE LEFT

FOR HELPING
thoughts
BECOME
words

and BEST of ALL
for MAKING the journey FUN

For
TRAVELING
this crazy
ROAD of
life together

For EATING DESSERT after getting INTO shape

For
GETTING
IN shape

For LIKING
REST-STOPS

For
TAKING
THE scenic
ROUTE

FOR looking BACK at old TIMES

Friends ARE FOR MAKING new MEMORIES

Friends ARE FOR FUN & FABULOUSNESS

IT IS MY FRIENDS WHO HAVE
MADE THE STORY OF MY LIFE.
—Helen Keller

FOR *not*
NEEDING
any WORDS
at all